W9-APG-649

Written by Tammi Salzano
Illustrated by Lawrence E. Myers
Designed by Sheila Lutringer

an imprint of
SCHOLASTIC
www.scholastic.com

Scholastic and Tangerine Press and associated logos are trademarks and/or registered trademarks of Scholastic Inc.

Published by Tangerine Press, an imprint of Scholastic Inc., 557 Broadway;
New York, NY 10012

10 9 8 7 6 5 4 3 2 1

ISBN-10: 0-545-13832-9
ISBN-13: 978-0-545-13832-1

Made in China

Scholastic Canada Ltd.; Markham, Ontario
Scholastic Australia Pty. Ltd; Gosford NSW
Scholastic New Zealand Ltd.; Greenmount, Auckland

Journey through Space

The night sky is a cool place! It's full of stars, planets, moons, and so much more. People have studied the night sky for a long time. It's a way to learn about what makes up the *universe* (**yoo**-nuh-vurs). That's just a fancy word for all the stuff in space. We're going to take a trip through space to look at some of the neat things out there, so hold on—it's going to be a bumpy ride!

Words in *italics* can be found in the glossary on P. 48.

Galaxies

The universe has galaxies (**gal**-uhk-sees)—about 100 billion of them! A *galaxy* is a very large group of stars, dust, and gas held together by *gravity*. There are three kinds of galaxies: spiral, elliptical (i-**lip**-ti-kuhl), and irregular.

A SPIRAL GALAXY IS SHAPED LIKE A PINWHEEL. IT HAS ARMS THAT CURVE OUT FROM THE CENTER. OUR GALAXY, CALLED THE MILKY WAY, IS A SPIRAL GALAXY.

AN ELLIPTICAL GALAXY IS SHAPED LIKE A BALL OR FLATTENED GLOBE.

AN IRREGULAR GALAXY DOESN'T HAVE A SHAPE. IT'S LIKE A BUNCH OF STARS JUST HANGING OUT TOGETHER!

Constellations

The Milky Way is filled with constellations (kon-stuh-**lay**-shuns). A *constellation* is a group of stars that form a pattern. Constellations help us remember where the stars are in the sky. People who lived a long time ago made up the constellations. The ancient Greeks named most of the 88 constellations we know today. They used the names of their gods, heroes, animals, or important objects.

Some constellations are seen only in the northern hemisphere, or north of the *equator*. Others are found only in the southern hemisphere (south of the equator). Many are seen in both at different times of the year.

Constellations look different during the year. The Earth spins like a top and also moves around the Sun. This makes the stars look like they're changing position. But really, *we're* the ones who are moving!

Most of the constellations in this book are drawn to show what they look like during the year in the northern hemisphere. If you're in the southern hemisphere, the star patterns look like they're upside down.

THE BIG DIPPER IN THE NORTHERN HEMISPHERE
winter

spring

summer

fall

Aquarius
(THE WATER BEARER)

Aquarius is drawn as a man pouring water from a jug. People from long ago saw Aquarius in the night sky during the rainy season.

BEST SEEN: Both hemispheres, September–December

AQUARIUS IS PART OF A GROUP OF CONSTELLATIONS THAT ARE FOUND ALONG THE PATH THAT THE SUN TAKES THROUGH SPACE. THE CONSTELLATIONS ON PP. 5–16 ARE ALSO FOUND ALONG THIS PATH.

Aries
(THE RAM)

In Greek *mythology* (mih-**thol**-uh-jee), Aries was a ram with golden fleece.

BEST SEEN: Both hemispheres, October–February

MYTHOLOGY IS A SET OF STORIES THAT PEOPLE TELL TO EXPLAIN THINGS THAT HAPPEN IN THEIR CULTURE.

Cancer
(THE CRAB)

Cancer lived in the water with Hydra, a large water snake. Hercules (**hur**-kyuh-leez), a Greek warrior, fought Hydra. Cancer tried to stop Hercules by grabbing his foot, but Hercules stepped on Cancer and crushed him.

BEST SEEN:
Both hemispheres, March–May

Capricornus

(THE GOAT)

BEST SEEN: Both hemispheres, September–November

Capricornus is drawn as a goat with a fish tail. The Greek god Pan was half-goat. He jumped into the Nile River to escape a monster. The top half of his body stayed a goat, but the bottom half turned into a fish.

Gemini
(THE TWINS)

This constellation looks like two people standing next to each other. They're the Greek heroes Castor and Pollux, who were twin brothers.

BEST SEEN: Both hemispheres, January–April

Leo
(THE LiON)

In Greek legend, Leo the lion was defeated by Hercules.

BEST SEEN:
Both hemispheres, March–June

Libra
(THE SCALES)

Libra was named by the Romans and shows the Scales of Justice. It's the only constellation in this group that doesn't honor a living creature.

BEST SEEN: Both hemispheres, June–July

Pisces
(THE FISH)

Pisces (**pie**-seez) was named for Aphrodite (af-ruh-**die**-tee), the Greek goddess of love, and her son, Eros (**air**-ohs). The two were trying to escape a monster, so they turned themselves into fish and hid in the water. They tied their tails together with a cord so they wouldn't lose each other in the dark water.

Sagittarius
(THE ARCHER)

Sagittarius is drawn as the centaur (**sen**-tar), a half-man, half-horse creature in Greek legend.

BEST SEEN:
Both hemispheres,
July–August

Scorpius
(THE SCORPiON)

Scorpius is a scorpion that was sent to stop Orion (oh-**ry**-uhn), a Greek hunter, from harming the world's animals.

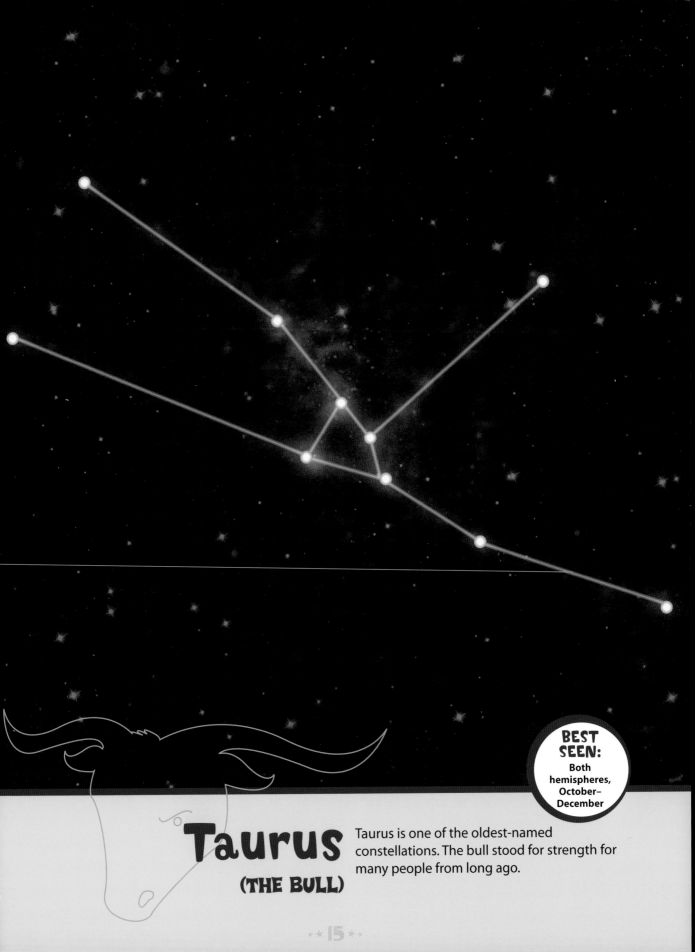

BEST SEEN:
Both hemispheres, October–December

Taurus
(THE BULL)

Taurus is one of the oldest-named constellations. The bull stood for strength for many people from long ago.

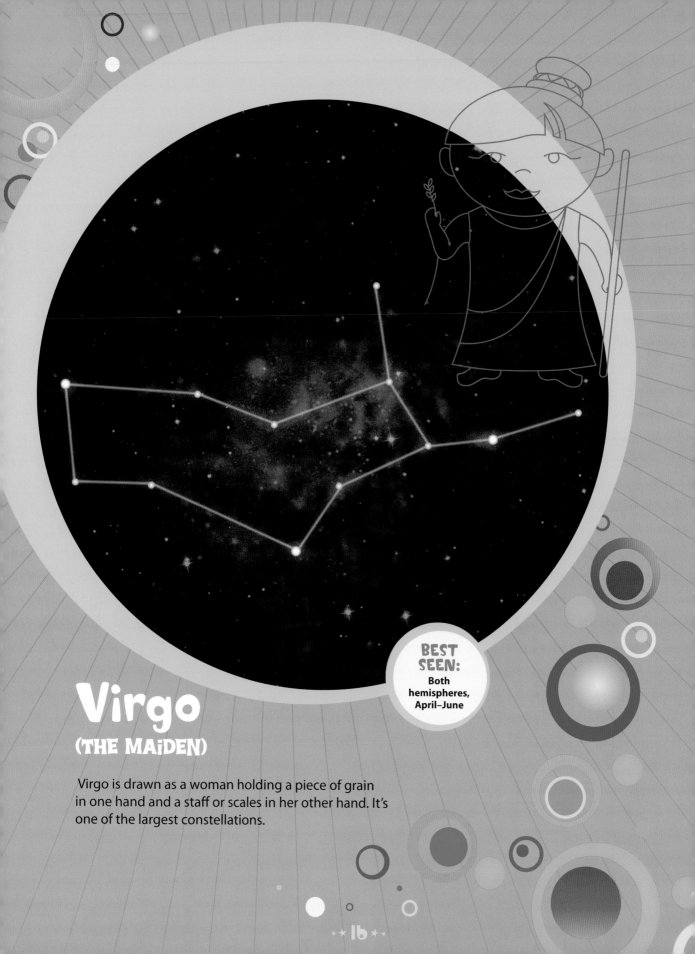

Virgo
(THE MAIDEN)

Virgo is drawn as a woman holding a piece of grain
in one hand and a staff or scales in her other hand. It's
one of the largest constellations.

BEST SEEN:
Both
hemispheres,
April–June

Centaurus
(THE CENTAUR)

Centaurus (sen-**tar**-iss) has the greatest number of stars that we can see with the naked eye (101). It honors the centaur.

BEST SEEN:
Southern hemisphere, May–July

THE CENTAUR IS A HALF-MAN, HALF-HORSE CREATURE IN GREEK MYTHOLOGY.

Crux

(THE SOUTHERN CROSS)

Crux is the smallest and brightest
constellation in the night sky.
It's surrounded by Centaurus
on three sides.

BEST SEEN:
Southern
hemisphere,
April–June

Orion
(THE HUNTER)

Orion was a great hunter in Greek mythology. The three stars that make up his belt are some of the easiest stars to spot.

BEST SEEN: Both hemispheres, January–March

Canis Major
(THE BiG DOG)

Canis Major is one of Orion's hunting dogs. Sirius (**sur**-ee-uhs), the brightest star in the night sky, is part of Canis Major.

SiRiUS

BEST SEEN: Both hemispheres, February–April

Canis Minor
(THE LESSER DOG)

BEST SEEN:
Both hemispheres, February–April

Canis Minor is Orion's other hunting dog. It's smaller than Canis Major. In fact, it's made up of only two stars!

Ursa Major
(THE GREAT BEAR)

Ursa Major honors a woman named Callisto (kuh-**lis**-toh) in Greek legend. It contains the Big Dipper, which is an *asterism* (**as**-tuh-riz-um).

BEST SEEN:
Northern hemisphere,
April–June

AN **ASTERISM** IS A GROUP OF STARS WITHIN A CONSTELLATION.

POLARIS

→

Ursa Minor
(THE LITTLE BEAR)

Ursa Minor, also known as the Little Dipper, is Ursa Major's son. Polaris, the pole star of the northern hemisphere, is part of Ursa Minor.

BEST SEEN:
Northern hemisphere, all year

POLARIS IS ALSO CALLED THE NORTH STAR. AS THE EARTH SPINS, ALL OF THE OTHER STARS IN THE NORTHERN HEMISPHERE APPEAR TO MOVE AROUND POLARIS.

Northern Hemisphere

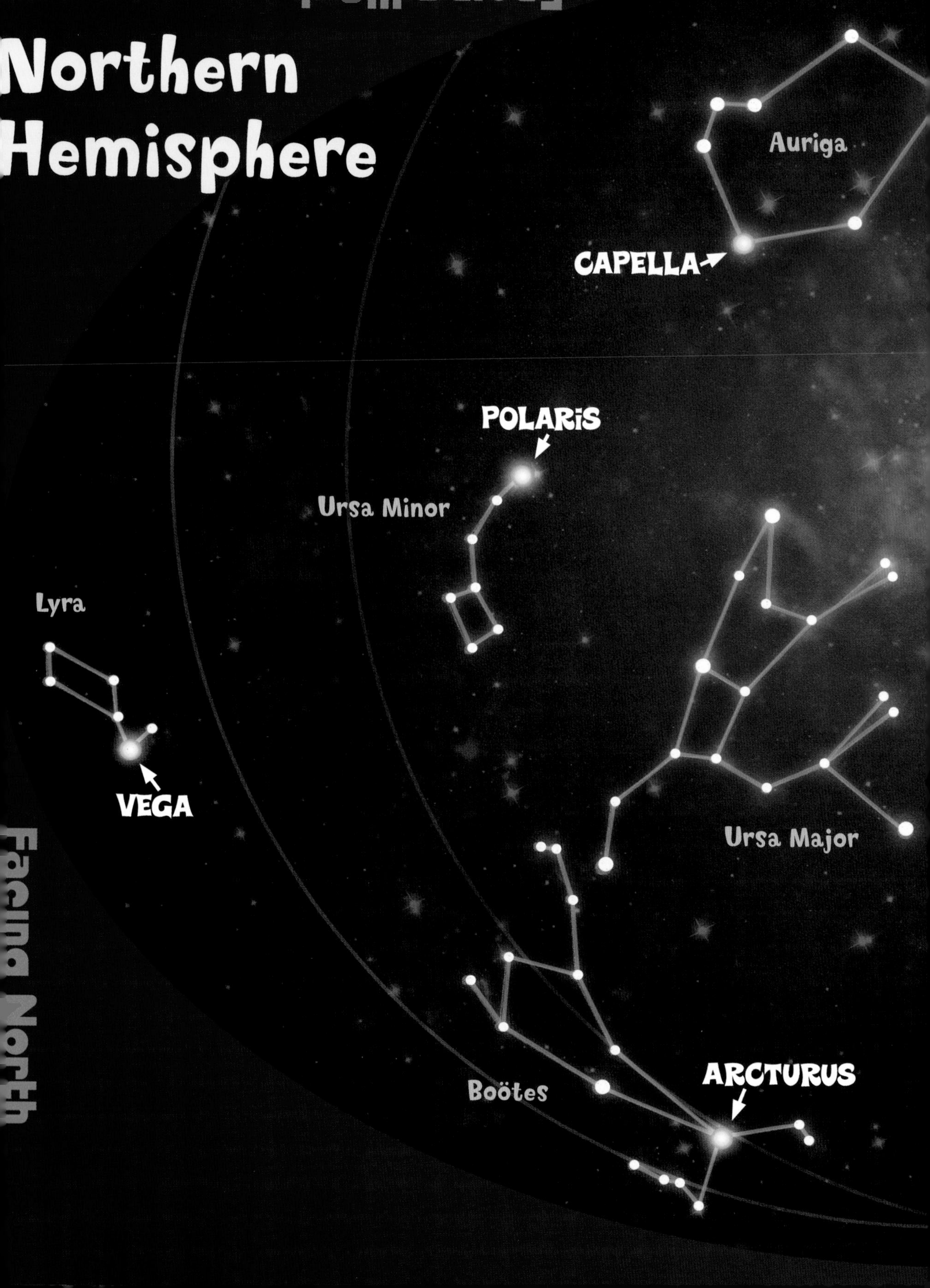

Auriga

CAPELLA

POLARIS

Ursa Minor

Lyra

VEGA

Ursa Major

Boötes

ARCTURUS

Orion

RIGEL

BETELGEUSE

SIRIUS

Canis Major

Canis Minor ← **PROCYON**

Facing South

Facing East

Southern Hemisphere

RIGEL

Orion

BETELGEUSE

SIRIUS

Canis Major

PROCYON

Canis Minor

Facing North

ACHERNAR

Eridanus

CANOPUS

Carina

BETA CENTAURI

Crux

ALPHA CENTAURI

Cassiopeia

Cassiopeia (kas-ee-uh-**pee**-uh) was a queen in Greek legend. She bragged that she was more beautiful than everyone else. The god of the sea sent a monster to destroy her kingdom, and Cassiopeia was placed in the sky.

BEST SEEN: Northern hemisphere, September–December

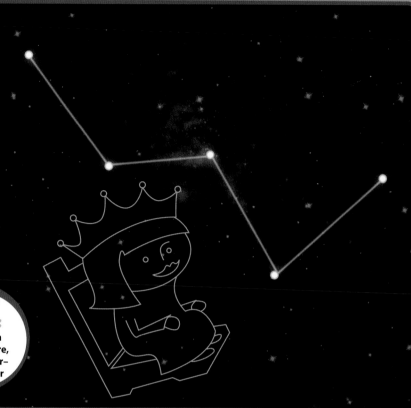

BEST SEEN: Northern hemisphere, October–November

Perseus
(THE MEDUSA KiLLER)

Perseus (**pur**-see-iss) is a Greek hero who defeated Medusa (muh-**doo**-suh), a female monster with snakes for hair. Anyone who looked at Medusa was turned to stone!

Andromeda
(THE PRINCESS)

Andromeda (an-**drom**-ih-duh) was the daughter of King Cepheus (**see**-fee-uhs) and Queen Cassiopeia.

BEST SEEN:
Northern hemisphere, October–December

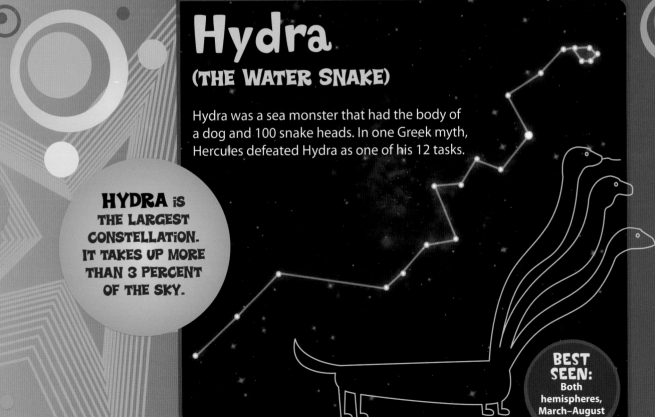

Hydra
(THE WATER SNAKE)

Hydra was a sea monster that had the body of a dog and 100 snake heads. In one Greek myth, Hercules defeated Hydra as one of his 12 tasks.

HYDRA IS THE LARGEST CONSTELLATION. IT TAKES UP MORE THAN 3 PERCENT OF THE SKY.

BEST SEEN:
Both hemispheres, March–August

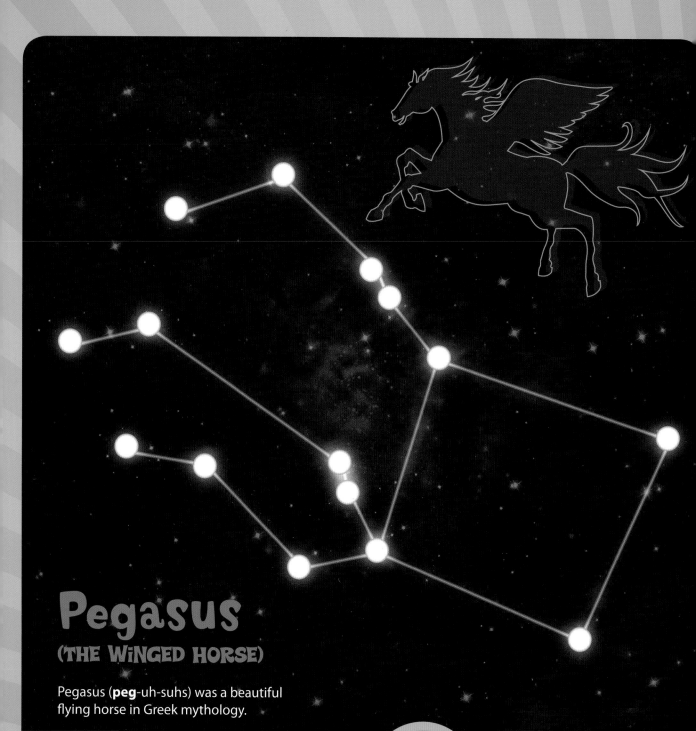

Pegasus
(THE WINGED HORSE)

Pegasus (**peg**-uh-suhs) was a beautiful
flying horse in Greek mythology.

BEST SEEN:
Northern
hemisphere,
September–
November

Boötes

(THE HERDSMAN)

Boötes (boh-**oh**-teez) was known by many cultures from long ago. In one story, he was placed in the sky to guard Ursa Major, the great bear.

BEST SEEN:
Northern hemisphere,
June–August

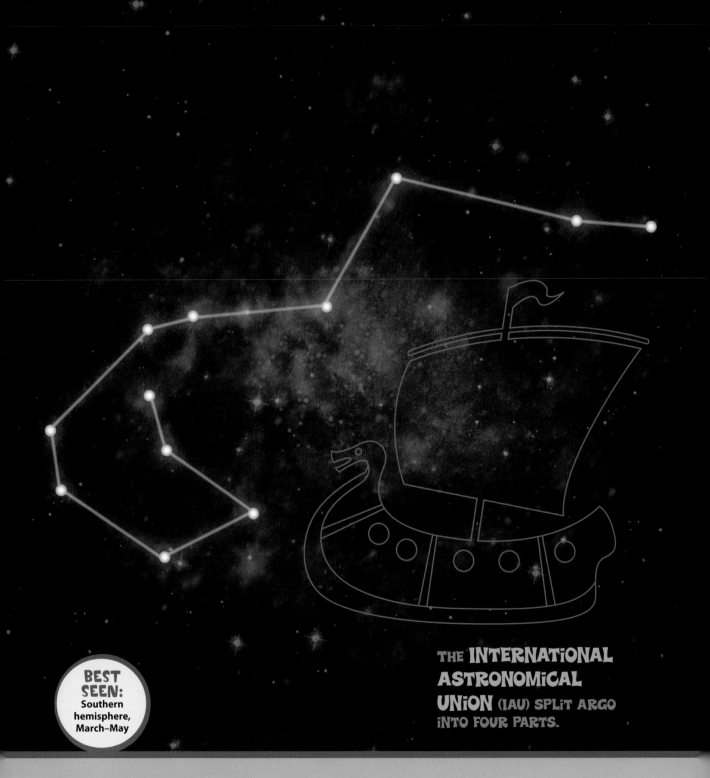

THE **INTERNATIONAL
ASTRONOMICAL
UNION** (IAU) SPLIT ARGO
INTO FOUR PARTS.

Carina
(THE SHIP'S KEEL)

Carina (ka-**ree**-na) used to be part of a larger constellation
named Argo that was shaped like a ship. Carina formed the
bottom of the ship.

Lyra
(THE HARP)

Lyra (**lie**-rah) is drawn as a lyre (**lie**-er), which is a stringed instrument like a harp. The lyre belonged to Orpheus (**or**-fee-uhs), who was a great musician in Greek legend.

Auriga
(THE CHARIOT DRIVER)

Auriga (aw-**rI**-gah) is drawn as a *chariot* driver with a goat on his shoulders and three goats in his arms. One Greek myth tells that Auriga was a man who couldn't walk very well. He made a chariot for himself so he could travel more easily.

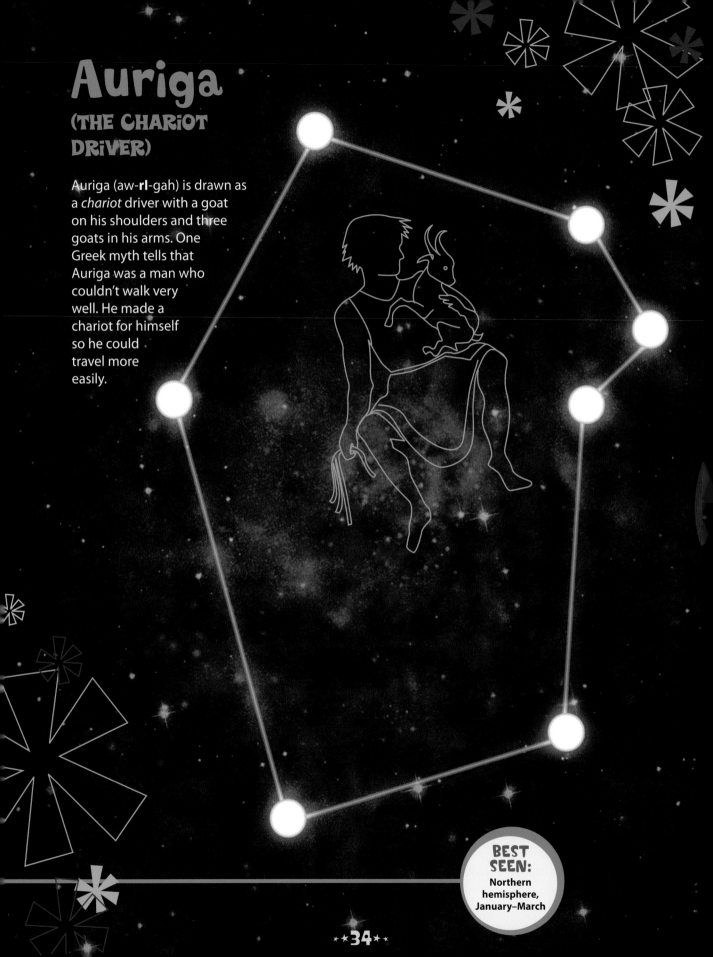

BEST SEEN:
Northern hemisphere, January–March

Eridanus
(THE RiVER)

Eridanus (ih-**rid**-in-uhs) is a long, winding trail of stars that looks like a river. It begins near Orion in the northern hemisphere and ends near Hydrus in the southern hemisphere.

THERE ARE BILLIONS OF STARS IN SPACE, BUT ONLY 10 OF THEM ARE THE BRIGHTEST OF ALL. HERE THEY ARE, LISTED BRIGHTEST TO THE LEAST BRIGHT. FLIP BACK TO PAGES 24-27 TO FIND ALL OF THESE STARS!

1. Sirius (IN CANIS MAJOR)
(ALSO KNOWN AS THE DOG STAR)

HOW TO FIND IT

First, you need to find Orion.

Find the three stars that make up Orion's belt. Look at the lowest star in the belt. Draw an imaginary line down and to the right to the brightest star you see. That's Sirius!

THE NAME SIRIUS COMES FROM THE GREEK WORD FOR "SCORCHING."

2. Canopus (IN CARINA)

CANOPUS CAN BE SEEN ONLY IN THE SOUTHERN HEMISPHERE.

HOW TO FIND IT

First, find Crux (the Southern Cross). Draw a line straight up from Crux to the stars in Carina. The bright star at the top of Carina is Canopus.

Remember that the constellations look different throughout the year. And if you're not sure where north (or south) is, ask an adult to point you in the right direction.

in the Night Sky and How to Find Them

ALPHA CENTAURI

3. Alpha Centauri (in Centaurus

Alpha Centauri is actually made up of three stars.

HOW TO FIND IT

First, find Crux. Look to the right of Crux for two bright stars close together. The star on the right is Alpha Centauri.

ALPHA CENTAURI CAN BE SEEN ONLY IN THE SOUTHERN HEMISPHERE.

4. Arcturus (in Boötes)

HOW TO FIND IT

First, find Polaris. It's the star at the end of the Little Dipper. Once you've found the Little Dipper, find the Big Dipper. It's a bigger scoop! Find the star at the end of the handle. Draw a line down and to the right to the first bright star you see. That's Arcturus!

ARCTURUS CAN BE SEEN ONLY IN THE NORTHERN HEMISPHERE.

5. Vega (IN LYRA)

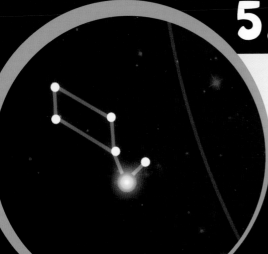

HOW TO FIND IT
Find the Little Dipper. Draw a line to the left and slightly down from the scoop to the first bright star you see. That's Vega, part of the constellation Lyra.

VEGA CAN BE SEEN ONLY IN THE NORTHERN HEMISPHERE.

6. Capella (IN AURIGA)

HOW TO FIND IT
Find Polaris. Draw a line up and to the right to the first bright star you see. That's Capella.

CAPELLA CAN BE SEEN ONLY IN THE NORTHERN HEMISPHERE.

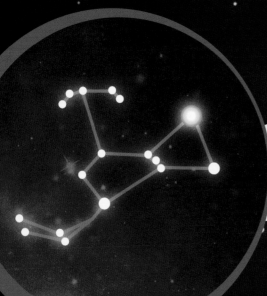

7. Rigel (IN ORION)

HOW TO FIND IT
First, find Orion. Now, find the belt stars. Look at the star that's highest on the belt. Draw a short line from that star up and to the right to Rigel.

8. Procyon (IN CANIS MINOR)

HOW TO FIND IT
Find Orion. Look at the three stars in the belt. Draw a line down from the belt to the first bright star you see.

9. Achernar (IN ERIDANUS)

HOW TO FIND IT
Find Orion and Rigel (Star #7). Follow the long, winding path of stars from Rigel; that's Eridanus. Achernar is the star at the other end of Eridanus.

ACHERNAR (A-KER-NAR) CAN BE SEEN ONLY IN THE SOUTHERN HEMISPHERE.

10. Betelgeuse (IN ORION)

HOW TO FIND IT
Find Orion and the three belt stars. Look at the lowest star on the belt. Draw a line from that star slightly down and to the left to Betelgeuse (beet-l-jooz).

BETELGEUSE

Other Space Stuff

STARS AREN'T THE ONLY THINGS IN SPACE! LET'S TAKE A LOOK AT SOME OTHER NEAT OBJECTS OUT THERE.

The Planets

Mercury

• Mercury is the planet that's closest to the Sun. It moves around the Sun faster than any other planet.

• The ancient Romans named Mercury after their swift messenger of the gods.

• Scientists have found water ice in *craters* (holes) at the planet's poles.

• Mercury's largest crater is 800 miles (1,300 kilometers) across.

Venus

• Venus is the second planet from the Sun.

• This planet is known as Earth's twin because the two planets are almost the same size.

• Venus is named for the Roman goddess of love and beauty.

• Its surface is covered with volcanoes. Some are 150 miles (240 kilometers) across!

crust
outer core
inner core
mantle

Earth

- Earth is the third planet from the Sun. It's the only planet known to have life on it.

- Our planet travels around the Sun at 18½ miles per second (30 kilometers per second).

- Earth is made up of layers. The outer layer is called the crust. Under the crust is the mantle. Under the mantle is the outer core. At the very center of the Earth is the inner core.

- Earth's inner core may be as hot as 12,600° Fahrenheit (7,000° Celsius). That's hotter than the surface of the Sun!

The Moon

- The Moon is moving away from Earth at a rate of 1½ inches (3.9 centimeters) every year.

- Tides in the oceans on Earth are caused by the Moon's gravity pulling on the Earth.

- In 1969, the United States landed a spacecraft, Apollo 11, on the Moon.

Mars

- Mars is the fourth planet from the Sun. It's known as the Red Planet because of the reddish dust that covers its surface.

- This planet is named after the Roman god of war.

- Scientists think there used to be liquid water on Mars. There are valleys and gullies on the planet where water might have flowed.

Jupiter

- Jupiter is the fifth planet from the Sun.

- This planet is named for the king of the Roman gods.

- Scientists think the Great Red Spot on the surface of Jupiter is a large storm.

- Jupiter is a gas planet. That means it's not solid, like Earth. Instead, it's made up of clouds of gases.

GREAT RED SPOT

Saturn

- Saturn is the sixth planet from the Sun. Like Jupiter, it's a gas planet.

- It's named for the Roman god of farming.

- Saturn is the second largest planet. Only Jupiter is bigger.

- This planet has seven rings. They're made up of billions of pieces of ice and rock.

Uranus

- Uranus (**yoor**-uh-nuhs) is the seventh planet from the Sun.

- This planet is a ball of gas and liquid.

- It's named after a sky god in Greek mythology.

- Uranus is tilted on its axis at a 98-degree angle. This means that the planet is lying on its side!

Neptune

- Neptune is the eighth planet from the Sun.

- It's named after the Roman god of the sea.

- Neptune's winds blow at speeds of up to 700 miles per hour (1,000 kilometers per hour).

- This planet can't be seen without a telescope.

Pluto

- Until 2006, Pluto was the ninth planet in the solar system. It's now known as a dwarf planet because of its small size.

- It's named after the Roman god of the dead.

- Pluto is so far from Earth that even the strongest telescopes can't see it clearly.

- In 2006, the National Aeronautics (air-uh-**naw**-tiks) and Space Administration (NASA) sent the New Horizons spacecraft to explore Pluto. The rocket won't reach Pluto until 2015!

Charon

- Charon (**kair**-uhn) used to be known as Pluto's moon. It's actually part of a double-planet system with Pluto.

The Sun

- The Sun is a star—a huge ball of burning gas in the middle of our solar system. All of the planets, their moons, and millions of space rocks travel around it.

- The Sun moves around the center of the galaxy once every 250 million years.

- The Sun was formed 4.6 billion years ago. Scientists think it will burn for another 5 billion years.

IF THE SUN SUDDENLY STOPPED SHINING, PEOPLE ON EARTH WOULDN'T KNOW IT UNTIL 8 MINUTES LATER!

Meteors

• *Meteors* (**mee**-tee-erz) are bright streaks of light in the sky. They're caused by pieces of space rock called *meteoroids* (**mee**-tee-uh-roids).

• Meteoroids fly through space all the time! When one hits the gases around Earth, it heats up and glows. Because it's moving so fast, the meteoroid looks like a line of light.

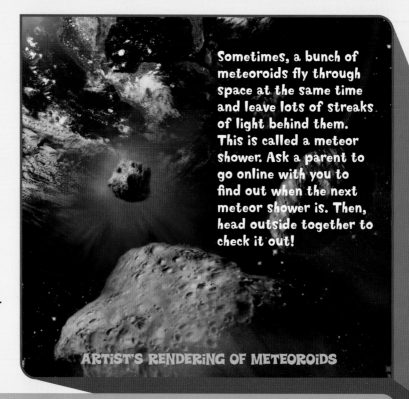

Sometimes, a bunch of meteoroids fly through space at the same time and leave lots of streaks of light behind them. This is called a meteor shower. Ask a parent to go online with you to find out when the next meteor shower is. Then, head outside together to check it out!

ARTIST'S RENDERING OF METEOROIDS

METEOROIDS THAT HIT EARTH ARE CALLED *METEORITES* (MEE-TEE-UH-RAHYTS).

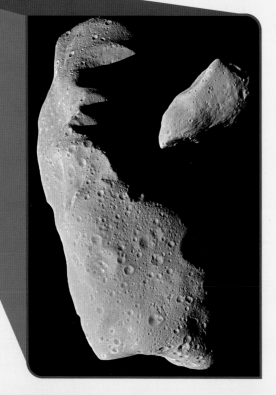

Asteroids

• *Asteroids* (**as**-ter-oyds) are space rocks that travel around the Sun.

• Some people think the dinosaurs died off because a large asteroid hit Earth. The asteroid caused big changes in the land, air, and water. The dinosaurs couldn't survive the changes.

ONE OF THE LARGEST CRATERS CAUSED BY AN ASTEROID HITTING EARTH IS IN SOUTH AFRICA. IT'S 1,865 MILES (300 KILOMETERS) ACROSS!